Book Introduction

Welcome to "The Politics of Possibility: Crafting a Vision for Tomorrow" — a journey through the realms of political imagination and innovation. In these pages, we embark on a quest to redefine the very essence of governance and chart a course toward a future brimming with promise and potential.

In a world often beset by political discord and disillusionment, it's easy to feel disheartened or disenfranchised. Yet, it is precisely in these moments of uncertainty that the seeds of change are sown. This book is a beacon of hope, illuminating pathways toward a more inclusive, sustainable, and prosperous tomorrow.

Through the lens of possibility, we'll explore the intricacies of today's political landscape, dissecting its challenges and opportunities with a discerning eye. Drawing inspiration from history, we'll uncover timeless lessons and wisdom that can guide us as we navigate the complexities of governance in the modern age.

But this book is not merely a reflection on the past or present – it is a call to action, an invitation to dream boldly and act decisively. With each turn of the page, we'll delve into the power of imagination, exploring innovative solutions and visionary approaches to age-old problems.

From grassroots movements to global initiatives, from technological advancements to environmental stewardship, we'll examine the myriad forces shaping our world and imagine new possibilities for collective action and progress.

Central to our exploration is the concept of inclusive governance – a philosophy that recognizes the inherent worth and dignity of every individual and seeks to amplify voices long marginalized or silenced. In our quest for a better tomorrow, no one is left behind.

Throughout this journey, we'll celebrate the diversity of human experience and the richness of our collective heritage. We'll embrace the transformative potential of collaboration and dialogue, recognizing that true progress is forged not in isolation but through the forging of common bonds and shared aspirations.

So, dear reader, as we embark on this odyssey of exploration and discovery, I invite you to open your mind and your heart to the Politics of Possibility. Together, let us dare to dream of a world where politics is not merely the art of the possible but the promise of the extraordinary.

Chapter 1: Setting the Stage - Understanding the Current Political Landscape

Welcome to the first chapter of "The Politics of Possibility: Crafting a Vision for Tomorrow." In this chapter, we embark on a journey to unpack the complexities of the present-day political landscape, shedding light on the forces and dynamics shaping our world.

The State of Affairs

Before we can envision a brighter future, it's essential to take stock of where we stand today. The current political landscape is marked by a tapestry of challenges and opportunities, intricately woven together by a myriad of social, economic, and environmental factors.

At the heart of many political systems lies a growing sense of disillusionment and discontentment among citizens. Trust in traditional institutions is eroding, as people feel increasingly disconnected from the decision-making processes that affect their lives. Issues such as corruption, inequality, and social injustice continue to plague societies around the globe, fueling calls for reform and renewal.

Globalization and Interconnectedness

In an age of globalization, the world is more interconnected than ever before. Advances in technology and communication have shrunk the distances between nations, fostering unprecedented levels of exchange and collaboration.

Yet, this interconnectedness has also exposed vulnerabilities, as economic crises, pandemics, and environmental disasters can quickly ripple across borders, affecting millions of lives.

Rise of Populism and Polarization

One of the defining features of contemporary politics is the rise of populism and polarization. Across the political spectrum, we see the emergence of leaders and movements that appeal to narrow interests and exploit divisions within society. This trend towards polarization threatens to undermine the very fabric of democracy, as dialogue gives way to discord and compromise becomes increasingly elusive.

Environmental Challenges

At the same time, we are facing an existential crisis in the form of climate change and environmental degradation. Rising temperatures, extreme weather events, and biodiversity loss are not just distant threats – they are urgent realities demanding immediate action. The political response to these challenges has been mixed, with some leaders embracing sustainability and others clinging to outdated paradigms of growth at any cost.

Inequality and Social Justice

Inequity remains a persistent issue in many societies, with disparities in wealth, opportunity, and access to basic services widening the gap between the haves and the have-nots. Marginalized communities – including women, minorities, and indigenous peoples – continue to face discrimination and injustice, despite decades of progress towards equality.

The Power of Hope

Amidst these challenges, however, there is cause for hope. Across the globe, individuals and communities are coming together to demand change and challenge the status quo. Grassroots movements, fueled by passion and conviction, are mobilizing for social justice, environmental sustainability, and democratic reform.

Looking Ahead

As we navigate the complexities of the current political landscape, it's essential to approach our analysis with both clarity and compassion. By understanding the forces at play and the dynamics shaping our world, we can better position ourselves to craft a vision for a more just, equitable, and sustainable future.

In the chapters that follow, we will delve deeper into these themes, exploring innovative solutions and visionary approaches to the pressing challenges of our time. Together, let us embark on this journey of exploration and discovery, as we seek to unlock the Politics of Possibility.

Thank you once again for your support and for being a part of our reading community. We can't wait to hear your thoughts.

Warmest regards,

Author Kashan Ajmeri

P.S. We love staying in touch with our readers! Feel free to reach out to us on Instagram @mkajmerismc for updates on upcoming projects and more!

Chapter 2: Lessons from History - Insights for Shaping the Future

As we journey through "The Politics of Possibility: Crafting a Vision for Tomorrow," our next stop invites us to turn the pages of history. This chapter is not just a retrospective glance but a voyage into the past to harvest wisdom for the future. History, with its myriad tales of triumph and tribulation, acts as a reservoir of invaluable insights. Let's dive in and uncover the lessons that can illuminate our path forward.
The Echoes of Ancient Governance

Our exploration begins in the ancient world, where the foundations of political thought and practice were laid.

From the Athenian experiment with democracy to the Roman contributions to legal systems, ancient civilizations have much to teach us about governance, citizenship, and the common good. These early political systems underscore the importance of civic engagement and the dangers of corruption and power concentration. By revisiting these ancient models, we can glean insights into the value of inclusive governance and the need for checks and balances in any healthy political system.

The Middle Ages and the Power of
Ideas

Moving forward into the Middle Ages, we encounter a time often characterized by feudalism and the divine right of kings. Yet, it was also a period rich in intellectual ferment, with thinkers like Thomas Aquinas and institutions like the Magna Carta laying early seeds for modern concepts of justice and individual rights. This era teaches us the enduring power of ideas and how they can challenge and eventually change entrenched systems of authority.

Revolutions and the Birth of Modern Democracies

The lessons from history become particularly poignant as we consider the series of revolutions that reshaped the world from the 17th to the 19th centuries. From the English Civil Wars to the American and French Revolutions, these tumultuous periods highlight the human yearning for freedom, equality, and self-determination. They remind us of the costs of ignoring the voice of the people and the potential for transformative change when a collective vision is pursued with courage and determination.

The Twentieth Century: Wars and Welfare

The twentieth century, with its world wars, cold wars, and struggles for civil rights, offers a stark reminder of the horrors that can ensue from ideologies of hate and division. Yet, it also stands as a testament to the resilience of the human spirit and the progress possible through cooperation and innovation. The establishment of welfare states, the decolonization movements, and the formation of international bodies like the United Nations exemplify humanity's capacity for empathy and our ongoing quest for a more equitable world.

The Digital Revolution and Globalization

In our recent past, the digital revolution and the forces of globalization have transformed the political landscape, connecting us in unprecedented ways and highlighting our interdependence. The fall of the Berlin Wall, the spread of democracy, and the rise of social media have all shown how rapidly political change can occur in a connected world. These events urge us to harness technology and global solidarity to tackle today's challenges, from climate change to inequality.

Drawing from the Well of History

As we reflect on these historical milestones, a few core lessons emerge. First, the quest for justice and equity is a constant in human affairs, requiring vigilance and advocacy. Second, real change often comes from the bottom up, through the actions of committed individuals and communities. Third, despite our differences, our shared humanity and common destiny call us to work together for a better world.

Looking Forward with Historical Wisdom

Armed with these insights, we stand better equipped to face the complexities of our own time. History teaches us not only about the pitfalls to avoid but also about the boundless potential of human collaboration and creativity. As we move forward, let's carry these lessons with us, drawing inspiration from the past to craft a vision for a brighter, more inclusive tomorrow.

Chapter 3: The Power of Imagination - Envisioning Possibilities Beyond the Status Quo

Welcome to a chapter that celebrates one of humanity's most extraordinary gifts: the power of imagination. In "The Politics of Possibility: Crafting a Vision for Tomorrow," we've traversed the terrain of our current political landscape and gleaned wisdom from history. Now, let's embark on an adventure into the boundless realms of possibility, where imagination is the key to transcending the limitations of the present and crafting the blueprint of a future we aspire to inhabit.

Unleashing the Creative Spirit

Imagine a world where the challenges that seem insurmountable today are addressed with solutions that are as innovative as they are inclusive. This vision begins in the mind's eye, with the courage to dream of alternatives to the status quo. History is replete with individuals and movements that dared to imagine a different world. Whether it was the dream of a nation founded on the principles of liberty and equality or the vision of a society where none would be shackled by the chains of oppression, imagination has always been the first step towards transformative change.

Beyond Conventional Wisdom

The power of imagination lies in its defiance of conventional wisdom. It invites us to question the assumptions and narratives that define our perception of what is realistic or achievable. In the political realm, this means envisioning governance systems that are more participatory, economies that are more equitable, and societies that are more just and sustainable. When we allow our imaginations to soar, we discover that the limits of possibility are often far beyond where we thought they lay.

The Role of Visionaries

Throughout history, visionaries have played pivotal roles in shaping the future. From visionaries like Mahatma Gandhi, who imagined and then actualized a path to India's independence through non-violent resistance, to Martin Luther King Jr., who shared his dream of racial equality and justice, these figures remind us that bold visions have the power to galvanize movements and inspire widespread change. Their legacies teach us that when imagination is coupled with conviction and action, the world can indeed be transformed.

Imagining a Sustainable Future

One of the most pressing challenges of our time is the environmental crisis. Here, too, imagination is key. What might a sustainable future look like? We can envision cities where green spaces and renewable energy sources flourish, economies that prioritize well-being over relentless growth, and communities that live in harmony with the natural world. By imagining such futures, we lay the groundwork for the innovations and policies needed to turn them into reality.

Technology and the Future of Governance

Imagination also propels us into new frontiers of governance and democracy. With the advent of digital technologies, we have the opportunity to reimagine how citizens engage with their governments and participate in the democratic process. From decentralized decision-making platforms to AI-assisted policy analysis, the potential to enhance transparency, accountability, and inclusivity is immense. The challenge is to envision and then create these technologies in ways that strengthen, rather than undermine, the democratic fabric.

The Journey Ahead

As we continue our journey through "The Politics of Possibility," let us embrace imagination not as escapism but as a vital tool for innovation and change. Let's challenge ourselves to dream boldly, to question deeply, and to envision a world that reflects our highest aspirations for justice, equality, and sustainability.

Crafting a Vision for Tomorrow

In the chapters that follow, we'll explore concrete strategies and actions to turn these visions into reality. But for now, let's take a moment to revel in the possibilities that imagination unfolds before us. For it is in the fertile ground of our collective imaginations that the seeds of a better tomorrow are sown.

Together, let's imagine—and then create—a future that transcends the limitations of today, a future where the politics of possibility becomes the foundation of a world we are proud to leave to future generations.

Chapter 4: Building Bridges - Strategies for Bridging Divides and Fostering Unity

As we journey through "The Politics of Possibility: Crafting a Vision for Tomorrow," we've explored the richness of our political landscape, drawn lessons from history, and unleashed the power of imagination. Now, let's delve into the heart of collaboration and unity: building bridges across divides that often seem insurmountable.

In a world marked by polarization and discord, the task of forging connections and understanding across ideological, cultural, and societal lines is both urgent and challenging. Yet, it is precisely in this endeavor that we find the seeds of a more inclusive, empathetic, and cohesive society. This chapter outlines strategies for bridging divides and fostering unity, guiding us toward a future where collective action and mutual respect define our political and social interactions.

Empathy as a Foundation

The first step in building bridges is cultivating a deep sense of empathy. Empathy allows us to see the world through the eyes of others, and to understand their fears, hopes, and dreams. It's about recognizing our shared humanity, even when we disagree. Strategies to enhance empathy include engaging in active listening, participating in dialogue initiatives that bring together people from diverse backgrounds, and promoting education that emphasizes emotional intelligence alongside critical thinking.

Celebrating Diversity

Unity does not imply uniformity. Rather, it's about embracing and celebrating the rich tapestry of human experience. Fostering an appreciation for diversity involves highlighting the strength that comes from different perspectives, skills, and cultures. Initiatives can range from community cultural festivals to inclusive policymaking that ensures all voices are heard and valued. By celebrating diversity, we build a common ground on the recognition of our unique contributions to society.

Constructive Dialogue

Constructive dialogue is essential for bridging divides. This means creating spaces where people can engage in honest, respectful conversations, even—and especially—when they disagree. Such dialogue requires rules that emphasize listening over speaking, understanding over persuading and finding common values. Workshops, town hall meetings, and online forums can all serve as platforms for this type of dialogue, provided they are facilitated with a focus on building consensus and mutual respect.

Collaborative Problem-Solving

Another powerful bridge-building strategy involves collaborative problem-solving. By focusing on shared challenges—whether local community issues or global crises—diverse groups can find a common purpose. Collaborative projects, such as community cleanups, educational initiatives, or joint ventures between traditionally opposing groups, highlight the practical benefits of working together and can transform adversarial relationships into cooperative partnerships.

Storytelling and Narrative

Stories have the power to bridge divides by illuminating the human experience in all its complexity. Encouraging the sharing of personal stories and narratives can foster empathy, challenge stereotypes, and build connections. This can be facilitated through media, literature, and public speaking events, where stories of struggle, resilience, and unity are shared and celebrated.

Leadership for Unity

Leadership plays a crucial role in bridging divides. Leaders who model respect, openness, and a commitment to unity can inspire their communities to follow suit. This involves leaders from all sectors—political, business, religious, and civic—working together to promote a culture of dialogue and collaboration. Leadership training and development programs can emphasize these values, preparing the next generation of leaders to navigate and heal societal divides.

The Path Forward

As we move forward, let's remember that building bridges is not a task for the few but a responsibility for all. Each of us has a role to play in fostering unity, whether in our interactions, our communities, or the broader societal and political arenas. In doing so, we not only enrich our own lives but also contribute to the creation of a more inclusive, understanding, and cohesive world.

The strategies outlined in this chapter are but starting points on the journey toward bridging divides. As we continue to explore "The Politics of Possibility," let's carry with us the conviction that, through empathy, dialogue, and collaboration, we can overcome the challenges that divide us and forge a future marked by unity and shared purpose.

Chapter 5: Empowering Communities - Grassroots Movements and Local Governance

In our exploration of "The Politics of Possibility: Crafting a Vision for Tomorrow," we've navigated the vast landscapes of history, imagination, and unity. Now, let's turn our attention to the vibrant heart of democratic life: empowering communities through grassroots movements and local governance. This chapter is an ode to the power of community action and the profound impact of civic engagement on the ground.

The Soul of Democracy

At its core, democracy is more than a system of government; it's a way of life. It thrives on the active participation of its citizens, not just during elections but in daily decision-making processes that affect their lives. This belief in the power of local action and governance is what fuels grassroots movements and community-led initiatives. Here, we explore how these movements emerge, grow, and ultimately shape the larger political landscape, bringing us closer to a world where every voice matters.

Grassroots Movements: Seeds of Change

Grassroots movements are born from the soil of community needs and aspirations. They start with a small group of dedicated individuals who share a common goal—be it environmental protection, social justice, or economic equality. These movements rely on the power of community organizing, where every meeting in a living room, every rally in a park, and every local campaign contributes to a larger wave of change.

Key to empowering these movements is the creation of open, inclusive spaces where everyone feels welcome to contribute. Strategies include hosting community forums, workshops, and social media campaigns that engage a wide audience.

Success stories from grassroots movements around the world offer inspiration and practical lessons on mobilizing community action, from neighborhood recycling initiatives that sparked global environmental campaigns to local human rights groups influencing national legislation.

Local Governance: The Power of Proximity

Local governance represents democracy in action at its most immediate level. It is where the rubber meets the road, dealing with issues that directly impact people's daily lives, such as public safety, education, and infrastructure.

Empowering local governance means ensuring that local authorities are responsive, transparent, and accountable to the communities they serve.

Participatory budgeting offers a compelling example of this empowerment in action. This process allows community members to decide directly how to allocate a portion of public funds, ensuring that their priorities and needs are directly reflected in local spending. Additionally, initiatives that enhance the capacity of local governance through training and resources can strengthen the ability of community leaders to advocate for and implement policies that reflect the community's desires.

Building Stronger Communities Through Collaboration

Empowering communities often requires bridging the gap between grassroots movements and formal structures of local governance. Collaborative projects can serve as a powerful catalyst for this engagement, fostering a sense of shared purpose and mutual respect. For instance, community policing initiatives that involve citizens in creating safer neighborhoods, or urban planning projects that solicit input from local residents, illustrate how collaboration can lead to more effective and sustainable solutions.

Technology as a Tool for Empowerment

In today's digital age, technology offers unprecedented opportunities for empowering communities. From apps that connect volunteers with local NGOs to platforms that allow residents to report issues directly to their local government, technology can enhance civic engagement and make local governance more accessible and responsive. Highlighting examples of technology-driven community projects underscores the potential of digital tools to amplify voices and mobilize action at the grassroots level.

The Journey Ahead

As we continue to navigate the path of possibility, the empowerment of communities through grassroots movements and local governance stands as a beacon of hope and action. It reminds us that change often starts with the smallest of steps, in the most local of settings, and that each of us has the power to make a difference.

By investing in our communities, fostering civic engagement, and nurturing the partnership between grassroots movements and local governance, we can build a more democratic, inclusive, and vibrant society. Let's carry forward the lessons and inspirations from this chapter as we forge a path toward a future where every community is empowered to shape its destiny.

Chapter 6: Technology and Governance - Harnessing Innovation for Positive Change

Welcome to a chapter that paints the horizon with the bright colors of hope and innovation. As we journey through "The Politics of Possibility: Crafting a Vision for Tomorrow," we've explored the realms of history, imagination, unity, and community empowerment. Now, let's delve into the dynamic interplay between technology and governance, a realm where innovation holds the key to transformative change.

The Digital Age: A New Frontier in Governance

We live in an era where technology reshapes the way we live, work, and interact. The digital age has brought about unprecedented changes, offering both challenges and opportunities for governance. This chapter celebrates the potential of technology to enhance democratic participation, streamline government operations, and foster a more informed and engaged citizenry.

E-Government: Making Public Services More Accessible

The concept of e-government encapsulates the use of digital tools to provide public services efficiently and transparently. Imagine renewing your passport or applying for permits without the dreaded wait in long lines, or accessing social services with the click of a button. Through websites, apps, and online platforms, e-government initiatives are making this convenience a reality, reducing bureaucracy, and making government more accessible to all.

Civic Tech: Empowering Citizens and Communities

Civic tech represents the intersection where technology meets civic engagement. It's about harnessing the power of apps, platforms, and digital tools to empower citizens to take an active role in their communities and governance. From platforms that crowdsource solutions for local issues to apps that facilitate voter registration and education, civic tech is democratizing participation and giving people a more direct voice in the democratic process.

Big Data and Analytics: Informing Policy with Precision

The rise of big data and analytics offers a groundbreaking way for governments to make informed, evidence-based decisions. By analyzing vast amounts of data, policymakers can identify trends, forecast needs, and allocate resources more effectively. Imagine targeting healthcare resources to areas most in need, predicting and preparing for environmental disasters, or understanding the real-time impacts of policy changes. Big data and analytics are turning these possibilities into realities, ushering in a new era of precision in policy-making.

Blockchain: A New Paradigm for Trust and Transparency

Blockchain technology, best known for underpinning cryptocurrencies, holds transformative potential for governance. Its ability to create secure, transparent, and tamper-proof records offers a new paradigm for public trust. From ensuring the integrity of elections to streamlining property registration processes, blockchain can safeguard democratic processes and reduce corruption, fostering a governance landscape where trust and transparency are paramount.

Artificial Intelligence: Shaping the Future of Public Policy

Artificial intelligence (AI) is not just a buzzword—it's a tool that can revolutionize governance. AI applications, from predictive policing to personalized education programs, can enhance public services and policy outcomes. However, embracing AI also requires navigating ethical considerations, ensuring that technology serves the public good, respects privacy, and promotes fairness.

The Road Ahead: Challenges and Opportunities

As we harness technology for positive change, we also face challenges, including digital divides, privacy concerns, and the need for robust cybersecurity measures. Navigating these challenges requires a collaborative approach, bringing together governments, tech innovators, and citizens to shape a future where technology enhances democracy and governance.

Conclusion: A Call to Action

The interplay between technology and governance offers a frontier of possibilities for enhancing democratic participation, streamlining public services, and making government more accountable. As we venture further into the digital age, let's embrace these opportunities with optimism and a commitment to ensuring that technology serves as a force for good, empowering citizens and strengthening the fabric of our democratic societies.

Together, let's shape a future where innovation and governance walk hand in hand, paving the way for a world that truly embodies the politics of possibility.

Chapter 7: Environmental Imperatives - Integrating Sustainability into Political Agendas

In our journey through "The Politics of Possibility: Crafting a Vision for Tomorrow," we've traversed the landscapes of history, imagination, unity, community empowerment, and the digital frontier. Now, let's turn our gaze toward our planet, focusing on the environmental imperatives that call for integrating sustainability into our political agendas. This chapter is an invitation to consider our collective home—not as a backdrop to human activity but as a central character in our shared story, deserving of care, respect, and protection.

Recognizing Our Shared Home

The Earth is not just a collection of resources to be exploited but a complex, living system that sustains all forms of life. The environmental challenges we face—climate change, biodiversity loss, pollution, and water scarcity—are not merely technical issues but deeply political ones. They demand a reevaluation of how we govern, how we live, and how we envision the future. Integrating sustainability into political agendas isn't just about policy changes; it's about nurturing a profound sense of responsibility towards our planet and future generations.

The Urgency of Climate Action

Climate change represents the most pressing environmental imperative of our time. Its impacts are wide-ranging and indiscriminate, affecting every corner of the globe. Political agendas must prioritize ambitious climate action that aligns with scientific recommendations to limit global warming. This involves transitioning to renewable energy sources, investing in green technologies, and enforcing regulations on emissions. However, it's equally about fostering global cooperation, as climate change knows no borders. The stories of small island nations facing rising sea levels or communities ravaged by extreme weather remind us that climate action is a moral imperative, urging immediate and collective efforts.

Biodiversity: Our Living Tapestry

Biodiversity—the rich variety of life on Earth—is under threat like never before. From the deforestation of the Amazon to the bleaching of coral reefs, the loss of biodiversity undermines the very systems that sustain life. Political agendas must advocate for the protection and restoration of natural habitats, enforce against illegal wildlife trade, and support sustainable agriculture and fishing practices. Embracing biodiversity is not just about conservation; it's about recognizing our place within a more-than-human world and ensuring that our actions contribute to its flourishing.

Pollution and Waste: Rethinking Consumption

Our consumption patterns have led to a planet clogged with plastic, air filled with pollutants, and landscapes littered with waste. Addressing this requires policies that promote sustainable consumption and production, such as banning single-use plastics, incentivizing recycling, and designing products for longevity and reparability. It's also about changing mindsets, and encouraging individuals and businesses to consider the environmental footprint of what they consume and produce.

Water: The Source of Life

Water scarcity and pollution pose existential threats to communities worldwide. Integrating water sustainability into political agendas means investing in infrastructure to ensure clean water and sanitation for all, protecting wetlands and rivers from pollution, and managing water resources in a way that balances human needs with ecological health. Water diplomacy can also play a crucial role in preventing conflicts, promoting cooperation over shared water resources.

A Green Economy: Prosperity within Planetary Boundaries

Transitioning to a green economy offers a path to prosperity that respects planetary boundaries. This involves not only investing in renewable energy and green infrastructure but also rethinking economic indicators of success. Gross Domestic Product (GDP) measures economic activity but not sustainability or well-being. Political agendas that embrace concepts like the Green New Deal or Circular Economy are pioneering ways to combine economic development with environmental sustainability.

Conclusion: A Call to Stewardship

Integrating environmental imperatives into political agendas is not just a policy challenge; it's a call to stewardship. It's about recognizing that we are part of a larger ecological community, with the responsibility to act in ways that ensure its health and vitality. As we continue our journey through "The Politics of Possibility," let us carry with us a commitment to place sustainability at the heart of our political discourse and actions. Together, we can forge a future where human societies thrive in harmony with the natural world, ensuring a livable planet for generations to come.

Chapter 8: Inclusive Governance - Ensuring Representation for All Voices

Welcome to a chapter that celebrates the diversity of human experience and emphasizes the importance of inclusive governance in "The Politics of Possibility: Crafting a Vision for Tomorrow." In this chapter, we explore the essential principle that every voice matters and the imperative of creating systems of governance that reflect and respect the full spectrum of identities, perspectives, and lived realities.

The Essence of Inclusive Governance

At its core, inclusive governance is about ensuring that all individuals, regardless of race, gender, ethnicity, religion, sexual orientation, or socioeconomic status, have a seat at the table and a voice in the decision-making process. It's about recognizing the inherent worth and dignity of every person and valuing the unique contributions they bring to the collective endeavor of governing.

Representation Matters

One of the cornerstones of inclusive governance is representation. This means having elected officials, policymakers, and decision-makers who reflect the diversity of the populations they serve. Representation matters because it ensures that the needs, concerns, and aspirations of all communities are taken into account when shaping policies and laws. From local councils to national parliaments, efforts to increase diversity in elected bodies and promote political participation among underrepresented groups are essential for building inclusive governance structures.

Engaging Marginalized Communities

Inclusive governance goes beyond representation; it requires actively engaging marginalized communities in the decision-making process. This involves creating spaces for dialogue, consultation, and collaboration that center the voices of those who have historically been excluded or marginalized. Initiatives such as community forums, citizen advisory boards, and participatory budgeting processes empower communities to shape the policies and programs that affect their lives directly.

Addressing Systemic Inequities

Inclusive governance also entails addressing the systemic inequities that perpetuate discrimination and exclusion. This includes policies and practices that promote equal access to education, healthcare, housing, employment, and justice. It also requires dismantling barriers to political participation, such as voter suppression tactics and restrictive voting laws. By addressing these root causes of inequality, inclusive governance creates a more just and equitable society for all.

Embracing Diversity in Decision-Making

True inclusivity in governance means embracing diversity in decision-making processes. It means seeking out and valuing a wide range of perspectives, experiences, and expertise when crafting policies and making decisions. This can involve establishing advisory panels or task forces that bring together stakeholders from different backgrounds, ensuring that policies are informed by a holistic understanding of their potential impacts.

Building Trust Through Transparency and Accountability

Transparency and accountability are essential pillars of inclusive governance. Openness about decision-making processes, clear communication of policies and their rationale, and mechanisms for feedback and oversight help build trust between government institutions and the communities they serve. Accountability measures, such as independent oversight bodies and mechanisms for redress, ensure that government officials are held accountable for their actions and decisions.

Conclusion: A Call to Action

Inclusive governance is not just a lofty ideal; it's a practical necessity for building a better future for all. As we navigate the complexities of governance in the 21st century, let us commit ourselves to ensuring that every voice is heard, every perspective is valued, and every individual is empowered to participate fully in the political process. By embracing inclusive governance, we can create a society that is truly reflective of the diversity and richness of the human experience, and that works for the benefit of all its members.

Chapter 9: Economic Reimagining – Redefining Prosperity and Equity

Welcome to a chapter that dares to challenge the status quo and envision a future where economic systems prioritize human well-being, sustainability, and equity. In "The Politics of Possibility: Crafting a Vision for Tomorrow," we've explored the contours of inclusive governance and environmental imperatives. Now, let's turn our attention to economic reimagining—an exploration of new paradigms that redefine prosperity and equity for the benefit of all.

Beyond GDP: Rethinking Measures of Success

For too long, economic success has been equated solely with GDP growth. However, GDP fails to capture many aspects of human well-being, such as income inequality, environmental degradation, and social cohesion. Economic reimagining involves shifting our focus from narrow measures of economic output to broader indicators of prosperity and quality of life. Metrics such as the Genuine Progress Indicator (GPI) or the Social Progress Index offer more holistic measures that incorporate factors like health, education, and environmental sustainability, providing a more accurate reflection of societal well-being.

A New Social Contract: Putting People First

Central to economic reimagining is the notion of a new social contract—one that prioritizes the needs and aspirations of people over profit. This involves ensuring that everyone has access to the basic necessities of life, including food, shelter, healthcare, and education. It also means guaranteeing fair wages, workers' rights, and social protections to ensure that no one is left behind. By putting people at the center of economic policies, we can create a society where everyone has the opportunity to thrive.

Sustainable Development: Balancing Growth and Environmental Stewardship

Economic reimagining recognizes that true prosperity cannot come at the expense of the planet. Sustainable development involves finding ways to meet the needs of the present without compromising the ability of future generations to meet their own needs. This requires transitioning to renewable energy sources, adopting circular economy principles, and promoting responsible consumption and production patterns. By integrating environmental considerations into economic decision-making, we can build a more resilient and sustainable economy that respects planetary boundaries.

Wealth Redistribution: Tackling Inequality Head-On

One of the greatest challenges facing economic reimagining is the issue of inequality. Economic systems that concentrate wealth and power in the hands of a few undermine social cohesion and democratic principles. Redistributive policies, such as progressive taxation, universal basic income, and wealth taxes, are essential for addressing inequality and ensuring that prosperity is shared more equitably. By narrowing the gap between the richest and the poorest, we can create a more stable and inclusive society for all.

Economic Democracy: Empowering Communities and Workers

Economic reimagining also involves democratizing economic decision-making processes. This means giving communities and workers a greater say in how businesses are run, how resources are allocated, and how wealth is distributed. Initiatives such as worker cooperatives, community land trusts, and participatory budgeting empower ordinary people to have a voice in shaping their economic futures. By decentralizing power and promoting economic democracy, we can create a more resilient and responsive economy that serves the needs of all stakeholders.

Conclusion: Forging a New Economic Vision

Economic reimagining is not just about tweaking existing systems; it's about fundamentally rethinking the way we organize our economies and societies. It requires bold vision, innovative thinking, and a commitment to justice and equity. As we continue our journey through "The Politics of Possibility," let us carry forward the principles of economic reimagining, working together to build a future where prosperity is measured not just in dollars and cents, but in the well-being of people and the health of the planet.

Chapter 10: Towards Tomorrow – Implementing the Vision for a Better World

In this final chapter of "The Politics of Possibility: Crafting a Vision for Tomorrow," we embark on a journey from imagination to action. We've explored the contours of inclusive governance, environmental imperatives, economic reimagining, and the myriad ways in which we can shape a better world. Now, it's time to roll up our sleeves and translate our vision into tangible, transformative change.

Building Coalitions for Change

Implementing the vision for a better world requires collaboration and cooperation across sectors, ideologies, and borders. It's about building coalitions of like-minded individuals and organizations who share a commitment to the values of justice, equity, and sustainability. By joining forces, we amplify our impact and create a collective momentum for change that is greater than the sum of its parts.

Advocacy and Activism: Making Our Voices Heard

Advocacy and activism are powerful tools for driving change at all levels of society. Whether it's lobbying policymakers for progressive policies, organizing grassroots campaigns for social justice, or participating in protests and demonstrations, every act of advocacy brings us one step closer to our vision for a better world. By raising our voices and standing up for what we believe in, we can hold our leaders accountable and push for the systemic reforms needed to address the pressing challenges of our time.

Engaging Communities: From Awareness to Action

At the heart of our vision for a better world are the communities we belong to—the neighborhoods, schools, workplaces, and social circles that shape our daily lives. Engaging communities involves fostering dialogue, raising awareness, and mobilizing collective action around shared goals. It's about empowering individuals to become agents of change within their spheres of influence, whether by organizing community clean-up events, starting local food cooperatives, or advocating for sustainable transportation options. By harnessing the power of community engagement, we can catalyze transformative change from the ground up.

Education and Empowerment: Nurturing Future Leaders

Education plays a crucial role in shaping the values, attitudes, and skills of future generations. By integrating themes of sustainability, social justice, and civic engagement into curricula at all levels of education, we can empower young people to become informed, active citizens and leaders of change. Educational initiatives, such as service-learning programs, environmental clubs, and youth-led advocacy campaigns, provide opportunities for students to apply their knowledge and skills to real-world challenges, fostering a sense of agency and responsibility for the world they will inherit.

Policy and Institutional Reform: Transforming Systems from Within

Implementing the vision for a better world also requires transforming the systems and institutions that shape our societies. This involves advocating for policy reforms that align with our values of justice, equity, and sustainability, whether at the local, national, or international level. It also means challenging entrenched power structures and working to dismantle systems of oppression and discrimination. By advocating for policies that prioritize the well-being of people and the planet, we can create the conditions for a more just, equitable, and sustainable future for all.

Conclusion: A Call to Action

As we look towards tomorrow, let us remember that the future is not predetermined—it is ours to shape. By embracing the principles of inclusive governance, environmental stewardship, economic justice, and social equity, we can build a world where every person has the opportunity to thrive, where the planet is cherished and protected, and where justice and peace reign supreme.

The journey ahead will not be easy, but it is a journey worth taking. Together, let us forge ahead with courage, compassion, and determination, knowing that the world we dream of is within our reach. Let us stand together as architects of possibility, building a future that honors the dignity and worth of every human being and leaves a legacy of hope for generations to come.

We'd Love to Hear From You!

Thank you so much for joining us on this journey through the pages of "The Politics of Possibility: We hope you found the Knowledge, insights, or stories within as rewarding to read as they were for us to write.

If you enjoyed your time in our world, please consider sharing your thoughts with others. Reviews help our book reach more readers and provide us with invaluable feedback, essential for our growth as authors.

Leaving a review on Amazon takes only a minute, but it makes a difference. Tell us what you loved, what moved you, or how this book has impacted you. Every word you write is deeply appreciated and carefully considered.

Thank you once again for your support and for being a part of our reading community. We can't wait to hear your thoughts.

Warmest regards,

Author Kashan Ajmeri

P.S. We love staying in touch with our readers! Feel free to reach out to us on Instagram @mkajmerismc for updates on upcoming projects and more!